Earth Day Birthday

by Pattie Schnetzler

Illustrated by Chad Wallace

A Sharing Nature With Children Book

Library of Congress Cataloging-in-Publication Data

Schnetzler, Pattie L., 1952-
   Earth Day Birthday / by Patricia L. Schnetzler ; illustrated by Chad Wallace.— 1st ed.
       p. cm. — (A Sharing nature with children book)
Summary: Set to the familiar music of "The Twelve Days of Christmas", verses describe different animals that illustrate the wonders of the wild world. Includes a factual section about Earth Day and ways to celebrate it.
   ISBN 1-58469-053-4 (hardback) — ISBN 1-58469-054-2 (pbk.)
   1. Children's songs, English—United States—Texts. [1. Earth Day—Songs and music. 2. Animals—Songs and music. 3. Songs.] I. Wallace, Chad, ill. II. Title. III. Series.
   PZ8.3.S29719Ear 2004
   782.42—dc22

                          2003018446

Dawn Publications
12402 Bitney Springs Road
Nevada City, CA 95959
800-545-7475
nature@dawnpub.com

Printed in Korea

10 9 8 7 6 5 4 3 2 1
First Edition
Design and computer production by Menagerie

Earth Day

Birthday

by Pattie Schnetzler
Illustrated by Chad Wallace

Dawn Publications

On the **first** Earth Day Birthday
the wide world gave to me . . .

*A bald eagle
in a blue sky.*

On the **second** Earth Day Birthday
the wide world gave to me . . .

Two grizzlies sleeping

and a bald eagle in a blue sky.

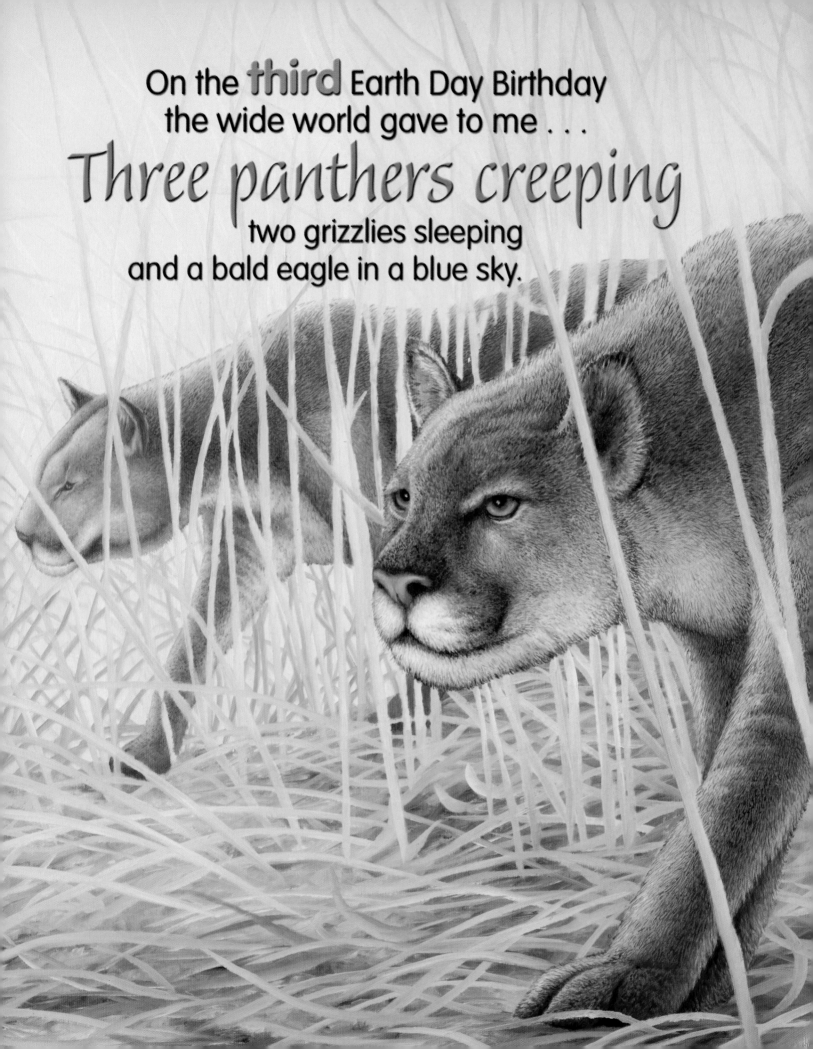

On the **third** Earth Day Birthday
the wide world gave to me . . .
Three panthers creeping
two grizzlies sleeping
and a bald eagle in a blue sky.

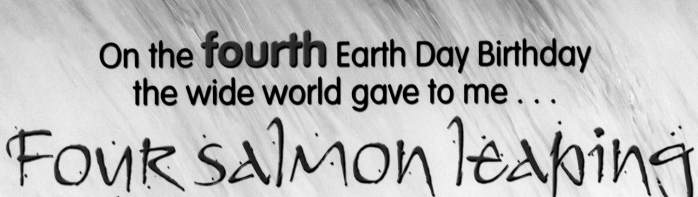

On the **fourth** Earth Day Birthday
the wide world gave to me . . . .

Four salmon leaping

three panthers creeping
two grizzlies sleeping
and a bald eagle in a blue sky.

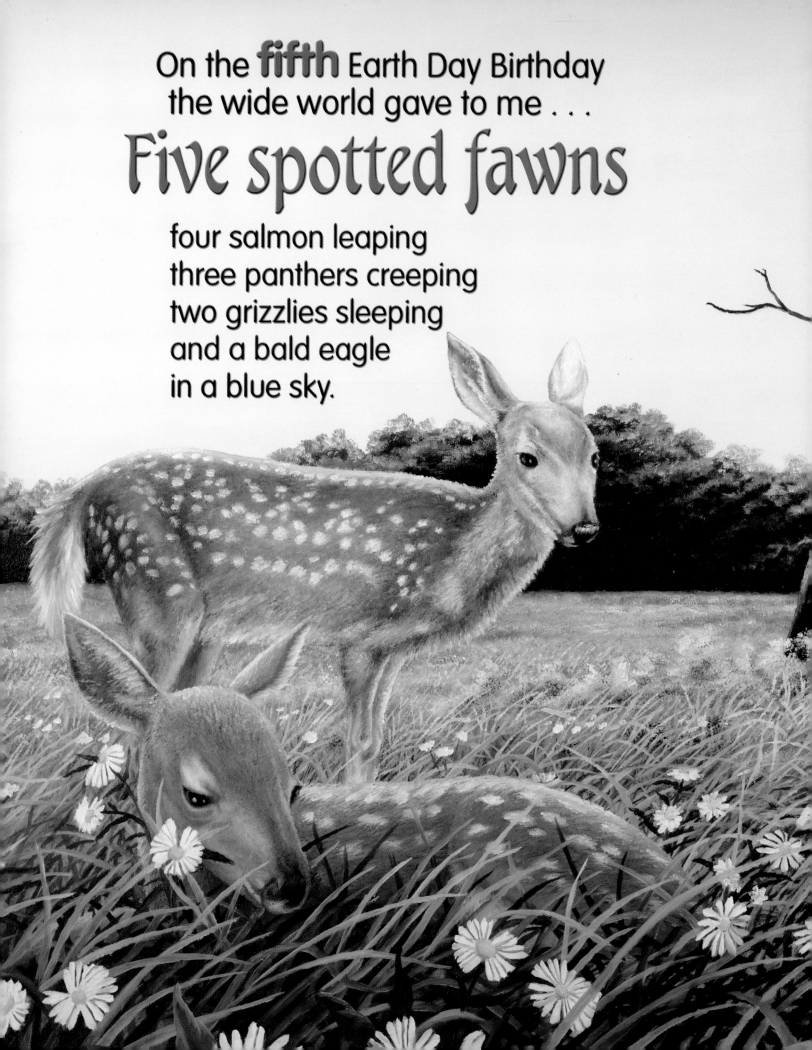

On the **fifth** Earth Day Birthday
the wide world gave to me . . .

Five spotted fawns

four salmon leaping
three panthers creeping
two grizzlies sleeping
and a bald eagle
in a blue sky.

On the **sixth** Earth Day Birthday
the wide world gave to me . . .

Six owls a-hooting

five spotted fawns
four salmon leaping
three panthers creeping
two grizzlies sleeping
and a bald eagle
in a blue sky.

On the **seventh** Earth Day Birthday
the wide world gave to me . . .
Seven whales a-breaching

six owls a-hooting
five spotted fawns
four salmon leaping
three panthers creeping
two grizzlies sleeping
and a bald eagle in a blue sky.

On the **eighth** Earth Day Birthday
the wide world gave to me . . .
Eight cranes a-dancing
seven whales a-breaching
six owls a-hooting
five spotted fawns
four salmon leaping
three panthers creeping
two grizzlies sleeping
and a bald eagle in a blue sky.

On the **ninth** Earth Day Birthday
the wide world gave to me . . .

Nine turtles hatching

eight cranes a-dancing
seven whales a-breaching
six owls a-hooting
five spotted fawns
four salmon leaping
three panthers creeping
two grizzlies sleeping
and a bald eagle in a blue sky.

On the **tenth** Earth Day Birthday
the wide world gave to me . . .

TEN BISON GRAZING

nine turtles hatching
eight cranes a-dancing
seven whales a-breaching
six owls a-hooting
five spotted fawns

four salmon leaping
three panthers creeping
two grizzlies sleeping
and a bald eagle in a blue sky.

On the **eleventh** Earth Day Birthday
the wide world gave to me . . .

Eleven seals a-swimming

ten bison grazing
nine turtles hatching
eight cranes a-dancing
seven whales a-breaching
six owls a-hooting
five spotted fawns
four salmon leaping
three panthers creeping
two grizzlies sleeping
and a bald eagle
in a blue sky.

On the **twelfth** Earth Day Birthday
the wide world gave to me . . .

Twelve wolves a-howling

eleven seals a-swimming
ten bison grazing
nine turtles hatching
eight cranes a-dancing
seven whales a-breaching
six owls a-hooting
five spotted fawns
four salmon leaping
three panthers creeping
two grizzlies sleeping
and a bald eagle in a blue sky.

On the day known as Earth Day,
  as every day should be,
we care for creatures as our family.

Celebrate Earth Day!

Every year on April 22nd, people around the world celebrate Earth Day. It is a day to help our planet by taking care of the air, water, land and animals. It is also a day for giving thanks for all the wonderful things that Earth means to us.

The idea of a special day to honor and help the Earth started in the mid-1960s when a group of people noticed that Earth was in trouble. Air, water and land were being polluted. Many plants and animals were losing their homes and dying due to change in their natural habitats. Something needed to be done.

First, a group of people in the United States tried to let everyone know what was happening. There were rallies and parades. There were speeches and fund-raisers. Soon, newspapers and magazines printed stories. Television stations showed programs. Knowledge spread that Earth was in trouble.

Then some people decided to create a special holiday—Earth Day—to remind people to help the Earth. A day in spring was chosen because spring is a time of new beginnings, and Earth Day encourages people to think of new ways to make Earth a healthy place for all living things.

The first Earth Day was on April 22, 1970. Twenty million people around the United States celebrated. They learned about recycling, protecting animal homes and cleaning up pollution. Now over two hundred million people in 141 countries around the world celebrate. Earth Day has grown! But more importantly, Earth is being helped.

Have an Earth Day birthday party! What kind of gift would Earth like? Here are some ideas:

Collect a bag of trash. Get a garbage bag. Go through your yard, neighborhood, park or school and pick up litter. Recycle everything you can, and put the rest in a garbage can.

Plant a tree. Get a sapling (a baby tree). Find a good place to plant it. Be sure to water it.

Plant flower or vegetable seeds. Pick your favorite flower or vegetable. Collect seeds from a mature plant, or buy a packet of seeds. Plant them by following the planting directions. Follow the directions to care for your plant.

Put up a bird feeder. You can build your own or purchase one. Fill your feeder with birdseed. Hang it up where you can watch the birds from a window or your yard. You can make a list of all the different kinds of birds you see.

Write an Earth Day poem or story. Pick a subject about Earth. Write a story or poem about it. Read it out loud.

Compose an Earth Day song. You can sing "Happy Birthday" to Earth. You can also sing "Earth Day Birthday" to the tune of "The Twelve Days of Christmas," or you can write your own song!

Play an Earth Day game. Make up an Earth Day game to play. Teach other people how to play. Have fun!

Make an Earth Day birthday card. Draw a design about Earth on the front of your card. Color and decorate it. Write a greeting inside your card. Tell Earth something special. Be sure to sign your card.

Earth Day Birthday

sung to the tune of
The Twelve Days of Christmas

Traditional melody
words by Pattie L. Schnetzler

Pattie Schnetzler has always loved animals, nature and the outdoors, and loves to hike and backpack. She is a trained surgical nurse, but she dedicates much of her extra time to helping the Earth. In Aspen, Colorado, Pattie assisted several environmental projects associated with John Denver, including the Windstar Foundation and the Rocky Mountain Institute. She is a member of the World Wildlife Fund and The Ocean Conservancy. Pattie believes that "We have to leave a healthy planet for future generations. And, we can all help!"

Chad Wallace graduated from Syracuse University in 1997, and has since illustrated four children's books. This is his second with Dawn Publications. Chad has always felt close to animals and nature, which are the primary source of his inspiration. Chad seeks to draw and paint animals in a natural setting while at the same time presenting a new perspective. Bright colors and human-like emotions invite the viewer into an animal's world that is both admirable and entertaining. When Chad is not in his Westchester, New York studio, he spends time at Bear Mountain in a cabin by a lake.

A FEW OTHER NATURE AWARENESS BOOKS FROM DAWN PUBLICATIONS

Sunshine On My Shoulders by John Denver, adapted and illustrated by Christopher Canyon. This heartwarming adaptation of a simple, sweet song reminds one of fresh and free childhood days. The hardback edition comes with a CD of John singing this popular song.

Do Animals Have Feelings, Too? by David Rice, presents fascinating true stories of animal behavior, and asks the reader whether they think the animals' actions show feelings or instinct.

A Tree in the Ancient Forest, by Carol Reed-Jones. The plants and animals around and under a grand old fir are remarkably connected to each other.

Stickeen: John Muir and the Brave Little Dog by Donnell Rubay, is a true wilderness adventure that transformed the relationship between Muir and a dog.

The "Earth Series" by J. Patrick Lewis, **Earth & You-A Closer View; Earth & Us-Continuous;** and **Earth & Me-Our Family Tree,** introduce the major habitats, the continuity of life and the connections between animals and their environment.

Under One Rock: Bugs, Slugs and Other Ughs is one of a series by Anthony Fredericks that discovers communities of creatures in habitats that are sometimes right at your feet.

Dawn Publications is dedicated to inspiring in children a deeper understanding and appreciation for all life on Earth. To view our full list of titles or to order, please visit our web site at www.dawnpub.com, or call 800-545-7475.